G A R E T H   M A S S E Y

EARTH ANGEL

A Story of Poetry and Prose

Made in South Africa

ISBN:978-1-0370-1433-8

Published by the Author
Illustrations by Nathan Phillips
Typesetting and Cover by Kexastudio Publishing

When you feel like the world
Is pushing you away,
Lean closer.

CONTENTS

Prologue

She sat upon a riverbank,
The woman weeping at the sight of the world.
'Why? Why all this pain?' she asks.
'When will it change?
When will the world be healed,
When there is no hate,
And love is all that remains?'
Hearing the patter of tear drops
Upon the dew-glistened grass,
An angel appears.

He leans over her shoulder and whispers,
'The sound of your tear held the tone of your heart,
And the questions you ask are drenched in sadness.
I cannot give you the answers you seek,
Yet I shall show you what I can,
So that you may better understand
Why it is so important
That you still believe.
Do you see the flower just there,
The white petals growing at your feet?'

The woman nodded,
Wiping her sleeve across her wet cheek.
'Take it from the ground,' the angel sweetly said.
The woman did as she was asked,
Plucking the flower by its roots.
The angel leaned into her ear.

'Now tell me, what does it need to grow?'
'The sun,' she answered.
'Yes,' the angel smiled, looking up high.
'Today we are in luck, as there is not a cloud in the sky.'
'What else?' he asks.
'Water,' replies the woman.
'We are blessed,' the angel sighs,
'As the stream is full,
Flowing fast beside us.
You should place it in the water.
It is sure to grow then,
Basking in the sunlight as it drifts along the surface of the stream,
Content with all the water it could ever need.'
'No, it will not grow that way,' says the woman.
'Why is that?' the angel asks.
She takes the time to think.
'The soil,' she says after a moment.

'There is food within it that the flower needs.'
The angel smiles and nods,
His halo shining silver above his head.
'That is true,
But why did you not think of that at first,
When asked what it needs?'
'I had learned from young,' the woman replies,
'That water and sun
Are most important for a plant to thrive.'

The angel places his hand upon her shoulder.
'Ah, the sun, how big and bright it is,'
says the angel musingly.
How can we forget such a star
That resonates with beauty and warmth.
And the water is all around us.
It is the rain that falls,
It is the rivers and the oceans.
Yet what you call a mineral,
So small that you cannot see,
Is no less important for a flower or a tree.'

The woman felt at peace,
Cradling the flower in her hand,
But she sighs and says,
'It's no longer able to thrive.'
'It will in you,' replies the angel.

'Let it rest behind your ear,
And when you leave,
Think on all that
Which many do not see.
Yet they still hope,
They still pray

... For the world to one day be
All that they believe.'

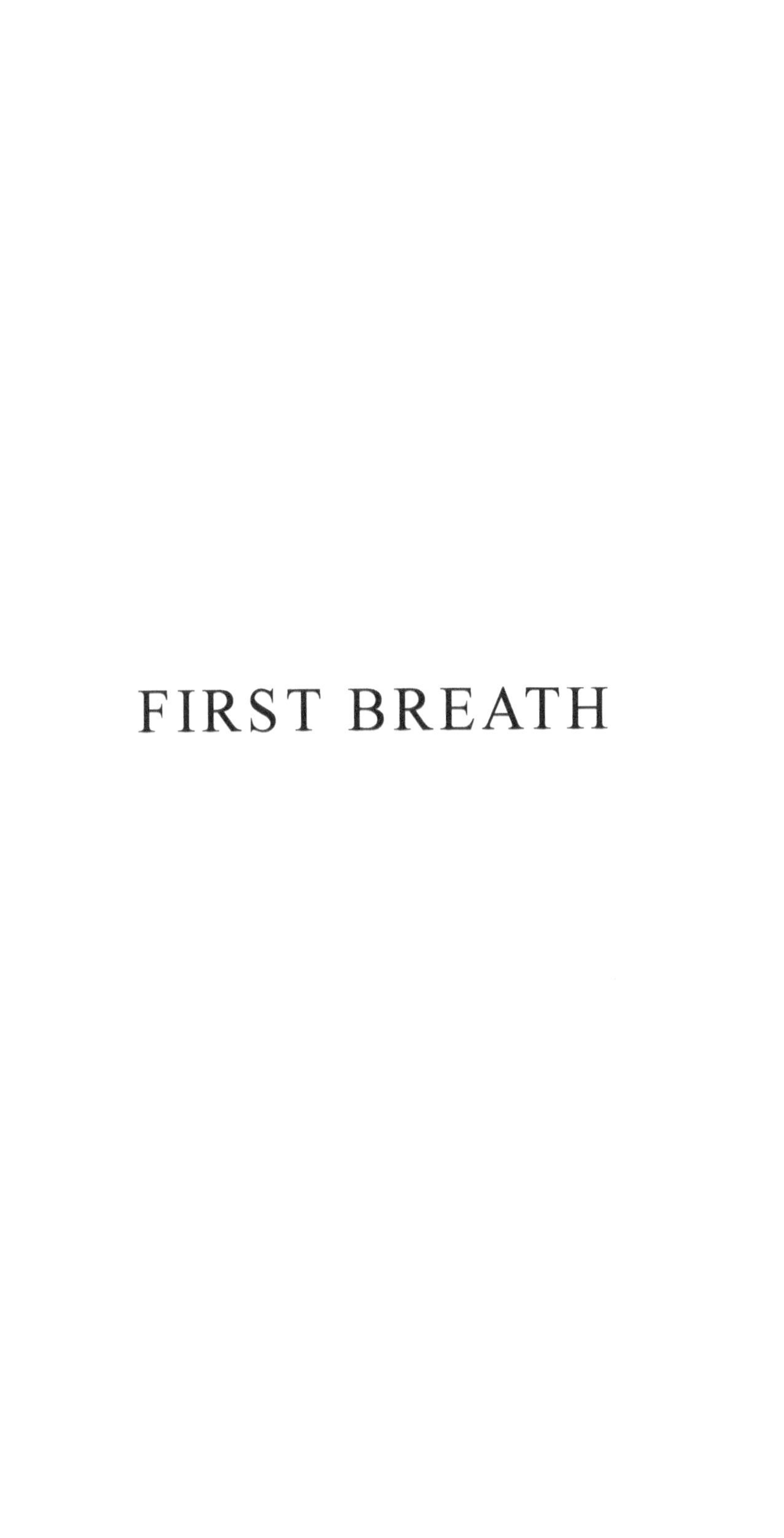

FIRST BREATH

How kind her heart is,
How courageous it cares.
I take it up in my palms,
Polished sun-kissed gold.
There is not a mark,
Not a smudge,
New as the day it was given,
A gift from her mother.
How beautiful she is,
How radiant she shines,

    All a glimmer
        with the glamour
            of giving.

Seep into those precious parts of you.
Within the stillness,
Your intuition awakes,
A spirit stirs,
calling to you.
Your mind leans to the sound,
Nestled in the silence,
A head on a lover's chest,
Intimate knowledge of every beat

... Wisdom without words.

There is a difference
between being alone
And being lonely.
One can wallow in loss,
Stagnant with despair
And desperate longing.
She is lonely.
Or one can contemplate in silence,
Her inner truths reflected
In the beauty that surrounds her.
She is alone,

Yet never lonely.

If a tree should be cut down,
May it become a book,
And within its aged bark,
A timeless tale is engraved,
Of love,
Of pain,
Of life.
It shall put down deep roots of emotion,
And in that way,
The tree will live on forever,
Basking in the light of your inspired heart.

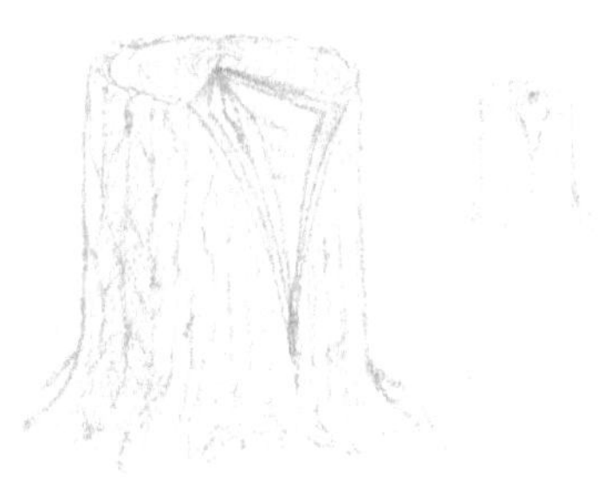

I knew a soldier,
 Who like so many feared his past
  —a young boy afraid of the dark.
   With each dream he saw their faces,
    The brothers and sisters he had lost,
     Their eyes closed,
      Cheeks pale,
       Hung like skew portraits
        On the crumbling walls of his war-torn mind.
         Feeling as though he had no choice,
          He took them down,
           One by one,
            Night by night,
             Dream by dream,
              Wrapping them in brown paper and twine,
               Tucking them beneath his bed
                —the ghosts of his past that might leave him be
                if he did not peek.

Yet he did not find his peace,
Tossing and turning,
The fear of forgetting his friends
Far worse than remembering their death.
And knowing he could not hide from the battle within,
He pulled them out from beneath his bed,
One by one,
Night by night,
Dream by dream,
Nailing them back up,
Straightened smiles covering
The patches of his battered past.
Their eyes were now open,
Beaming proud as they were before the fight,
Faces blushed with color,
Aglow with life.
He left them there,
Never to take them down again,
Fearing the dark a little less.

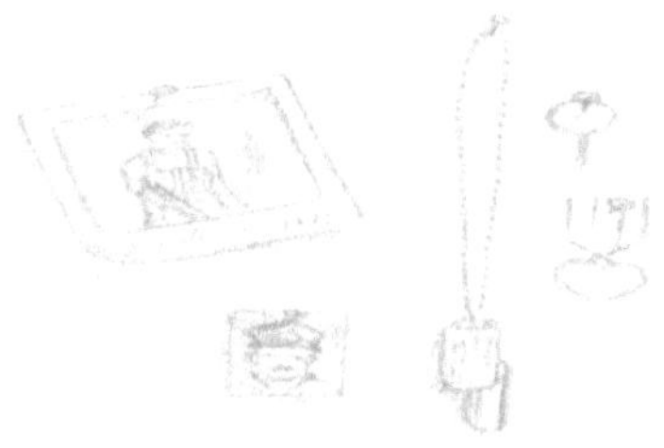

A great flame
Burns within you,
Possessing the power
To forge pain
Into beauty
... Create your masterpiece.

21

Tying one of my
Heartstrings to yours,
I attach paper cups to the ends,
And together,
Childlike in love,
We listen to every beat.

I hope that when you
Grace others with your light,
It shines with your true colors
… Each and every shade of the spectrum.

23

Why do they say
The wind moans,
When simply it is
Singing an eerie call
To its one true love?
... The sea.

With every breath
You prove
That something
As miraculous
As life
Can come true.
You are
The impossible magic
That the universe,
After all this time,
Was finally able
To conjure up.

I find comfort in the care of
my Mother Nature,
The sound of her rain
soothing my weary heart,
A lullaby of pitter-patter
upon leaves,
Singing me gently
off to sleep.

Let your life
Be a hymn of happiness,
But find the strength
To sing within the sadness.

27

A precious love,
One that is rare in display
But common in all hearts,
Is what we breathe for.
It can be given
Without ever giving it away,
Used yet never depleted.
I hope for you,
Dear friend,
To be rich in this way,
To possess an immeasurable wealth,
One that devils dream to ensnare
And angels spend eternity to protect.

Be kind,
Always,
And embolden those
Who fail to see
That they are worthy
To dream.

29

The wind whispered among the leaves,
Stirring the creatures of the night,
Chirping crickets setting the mood,
Playing their wings like violins.
And looking deep into her moonlit eyes,
I heard the hushed hoot of an owl,
A crooning teen at his sweetheart's window,
Confessing his love.

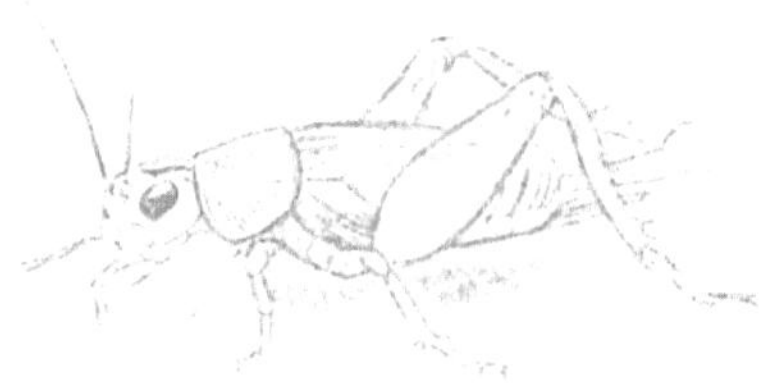

Pushing his tiny toy boat
 Out onto the pond,
  The little boy glanced to another
   Drifting toward his own.
    It belonged to a girl,
     Waving to him from the far bank.
     The boats sailed passed,
      A kiss of their bows,
       And as the girl softly smiled,
        Curling her teased hair behind her ear,
        The boy wondered if she,
         Like he,
          Also secretly wished
          For the wind
           To steer their boats
            Back to one another again.

'We are like them,
 These sailing boats,
  Facing the squalls of life,
   Hopeful that the currents are kind,
   Faithful that the mighty winds
    Will forever power our sails,
     Taking us back to the distant shores,
     Where a familiar figure
      Would be waiting upon a hill,
      A handkerchief in hand
       —the lighthouse of our love.

31

Always look at the world
Through the lens of love

... It lets in the most light.

A rose blooms,
Petals fold satin crimson,
Fragrant affection,
Stem cut clean,
Leaves still breath,
Thorns caution,
True love swoons
— emotion born from a seed.

34

The dark is by design,
To measure against
What we create
In light
And love.

*'How else could we sense
the beauty in the best of us?'*

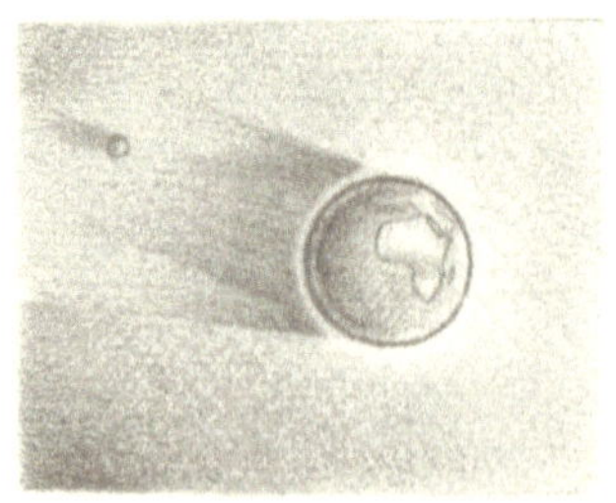

35

Sweet memories
Are phantom kisses
On the soul,
Still felt in the darkest hour,
Reminding us that love
Never leaves.

Seeing is believing
—so they say.
Yet I find believing is seeing.
Open your heart.
It has a clearer sight
Of all that lies
Beyond the eyes.

I have a memory of Mississippi,
Of a man I had met there once,
Sitting in a garden beneath the giant oak tree.
There was a meticulous modesty about him,
A calm and caring resolve for the time he had been given,
As he listened to the sound of the rustling leaves.
I sat down beside him on the stone bench.
His hair was long,
Curled silver strands
—Spanish moss swaying in the sultry breeze—
I gazed upon his face marked with deep lines
—thickened bark of an old oak tree—
Each groove a memory that the years carved away,
Creating the man that he had grown to be.
His hazy white eyes turned to me,
Blind windows to his soul,
But I could still see it shining clearly.
I leaned in as he softly spoke
—a little louder than the whisper of the wind—
And he told me of the tall tales of his youth,
The wonders he had seen.

The decadence of art,
Lavish spread of confections,
Honey-glazed hopes,
Puff pastry passions,
Whipped cream wishes,
Soul's sweet sensation,
Taking little bites,
A sweet tooth for life,
Delicate morsels delight,
Lips sticky with jelly donuts,
Powder sugar on noses,
Recipes penned from inspiration,
Secret ingredients of creation
... *Love.*

'Plate your art it as you wish,
Upon paper,
Canvas,
Or stone.
Food for the soul.'

Your words shape the world.
Wield them with caution.
Calm in their compassion,
Stern in their resolve,
Abundant in their praise,
Sparse in their critique,
And bold in their belief.

Love is blind,
A feeling the soul
Interprets by touch,
Like

    Fingers

        Drifting

          Across

          Braille.

They say the light we see from stars
May be from those that have already died.
Perhaps it is the same for the people we have lost,
Still feeling their love beaming bright
Long after they are gone.

FIRST STEP

If you are to wear your heart on your sleeve
Then pin your soul upon your chest.
Your heart like a soldier's stripes,
A symbol for all your loves.
Your soul like a pink ribbon,
Displaying what you stand for
… All that you *courageously love.*

I see the hidden depths of people,
Gathering up their thoughts
Like seeds of windswept dandelions.
Before I blow them further off,
Sending them back to the wind
—*not mine to keep*—
I stop.
I hold them a moment longer,
Admiring how they loved,
And how dearly they believed.

It shaped like a dream,
A deep encompassing night,
Glossy outlines of bowing land
—*a world made of moonshine and swelling shadows*—
A sweeping note of a cello string
Called calmly for home,
The desperate desire of a violin
Shuddered and wined,
Weeping and weary of hope,
Clinging to it in its final fading flare.
Two lovers passed messages in musical notes,
Whispering sweet longings by firelight.
A passion stirred beneath the stars,
Within the sights,
Within the sounds,

… The turbulent emotions of life.

When the rains cease,
I wander the desert of my heart,
Searching for the oasis of you.
And discovering your rare beauty,
I hold the life of you up to my lips,
Quenching my soul.

Hold onto that ancient wild of you,
Howling to wolves on moonlit nights,
The drumming of your heart beating bravely,

Fearless of what awaits beyond

    The waning warmth

        Of a dying fire.

Spread your love
Like a thousand paper lanterns
Across the night sky,
One for each grieving soul,
Reminding them of how a single light
Can burn so bright
Within something so fragile.

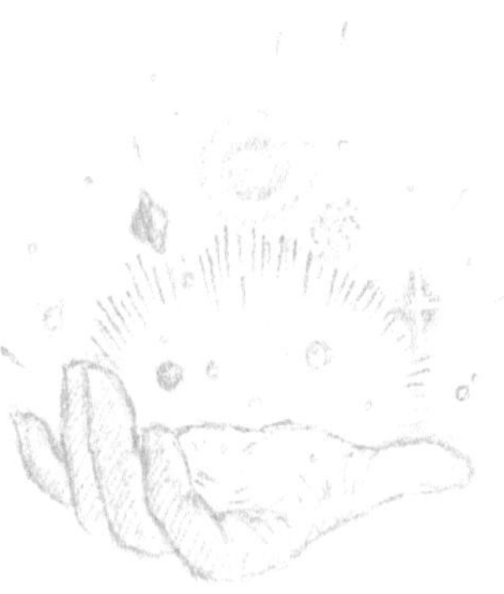

It is in the outer worlds of the mind
—that universe of endless imagination—
Where the soul creates.
And what is more true and more pure
Than to have that art fulfilled
Within those whose hearts we touch.

What an intoxicating
Sensation it is
To be
   Madly
     Inspired
       By
         Life.

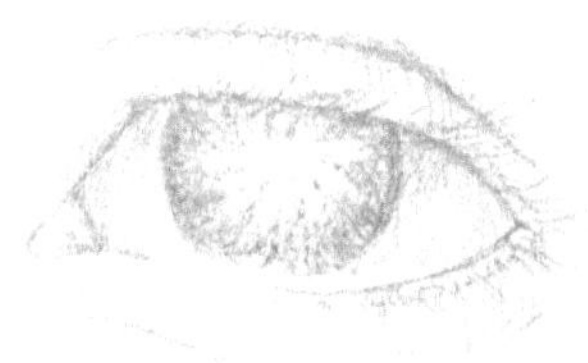

Always lean towards love,
And in those darker times,
When you feel like the world
Is pushing you away,
Lean closer.

An aching heart
Is but a soul in mourning,
And such a thing is meant to endure.
In time let it love again.

54

I have a vision for the future,
Taking great care in plotting my course.
I hold up a toy spyglass to the horizon of my dreams,
Turning the kaleidoscope,
A hundred colored crystals folding in the light,
A dazzling array of treasures to find,
Inspired by my inner child.

My soul is a kite
Upon the winds of life,
Guided by the subtle sway of God's hand.
He smiles at me like a curious child,
Adoring that delicate dance,
Keeping a weather eye
On a brewing storm.

56

Your pain is yours alone,
My friend.
No one can take that away from you.
I saw it there,
That great loss you suffered,
Behind the glimmer of your eyes,
Of all that was still alive.
A year has now passed,
My friend,
Since last we met,
And I see that pain still resides,
Those shattered bulbs,

Like silver splinters in your eyes.
But now,
There is something else,
Something there that wasn't before,
Those broken bulbs a flicker,
Lights fighting to survive.
And I do not doubt,
My friend,
That when next I see you,
Another year from now,
They will burn a little brighter,
A little warmer,
A little kinder.

At night,
When the day's work has come to an end,
When the desire for man-made riches is put to rest,
I dream of a world in which to simply view its wonders
Would be a great enough gift.
When the treasures in streams
Would not be of gold,
But shimmering fish,
A sight to behold.

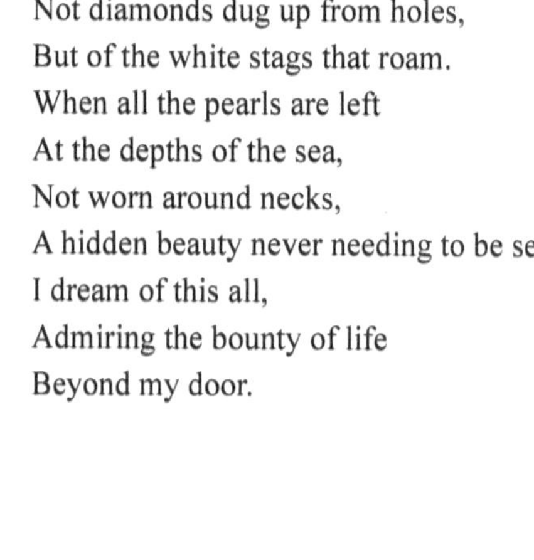

When the gems in the mountains
Would be found in its folds,
Not diamonds dug up from holes,
But of the white stags that roam.
When all the pearls are left
At the depths of the sea,
Not worn around necks,
A hidden beauty never needing to be seen.
I dream of this all,
Admiring the bounty of life
Beyond my door.

The course of destiny
Is chartered by the choices we make,
Not derailed from failures,
But steered by the growth
Of a wise heart.

The sky was a swirl of fine cloud,

      Twisting like strands of hair around a girl's finger.

It must have been Mother Nature peering down at me,

      Wondering if

          I

            had

               finally

                  found

                     my

                        way.

We are fortified by our faith in love.
What better armor to guard us against hate
Than a heart forged from the fires of compassion.
It shall be stronger and lighter than any iron or steel

... Wear it well.

Love

People speak about the unfairness of their lives, as if pain should be measured out and dispersed equally among all… in low quantities, as it would be preferred.

I think people have grown quite fond of seeing God as the almighty banker of the world, his scale filled with gold, able to tip it in their favor.

'Dear Lord,
would you please consider accepting prayers for pay?'
I imagine people to say.

'They must be worth something to you.
How many would be enough?'

So many fail to see that it is us who hold the power to tip the scales, to have the riches of joy sway in our favor. But first, God must not be seen as the banker but the scale itself, the great one of life that we must weigh down with love.

When the great epiphany of purpose strikes you,
It is the realization of your soul's calling.
You step onto that path,
The new beginning of you.
An inner voice is heard,
Guiding the way.
It is familiar to the you of old,
But clearer now.
No noise to muffle its truths,
No clutter clanging about your thoughts.

You feel freedom within that calming sound,
Not held sway by time.
No ticking of a cosmic clock,
Counting down each beat of your heart.
No weighing your worth by what others believe,
Bound by judgment.
You no longer anxiously count your steps,
Looking back to see how far you have come.
You simply move forward with faith,
Setting out on the great journey of YOU.

At times we must find comfort in frailty,
Knowing that it is only from fear
That we can muster the courage to overcome it.
We all have that warrior within us.
Let love be your greatest weapon,
Wielded with a mighty heart.

Peeking from behind a cloud,
God looked down,
Shaking His head at the squabbles
Between science and religion,
Like a father watching his two children
Playing in the same sandbox,
Arguing over whose castle was built better.
And loving them both,
God hoped that one day
They would see past their differences,
Realizing that what they had in common
Was far more important
—*passion for life.*

It is a curious
Wide,
Open land,
This life,
Where as far
As the heart can feel,
We search for love.
Reckless
And cautious
We tread,
Down valleys,
And over mountains
Steeped in emotion,
Witnessing
The splendor
And terror,
As through
Our joys
And pains,
The highs
And lows,
We flourish
And quake.

Take the time you need to grow.
The sprout of an oak seed
May appear as merely a plant,
Yet it is nonetheless the mighty tree
It one day will rise to be.

A mind
Submitting to failure
Is a heart
That has given up hope

... Do not stop believing.

FIRST LEAP

Even if something does not exist,
What is most beautiful
Is us believing that it can.
Such belief brings it to life within us,
And there in that emotion,
That inner world of perpetual creation,
It resides and thrives.
And maybe with a little faith and
—dare I say—

Magic,
It grows big enough,
Bursting at the seams of our imagination,
And spills out into the world,
Taking shape of something more…
Something beautifully *surreal.*

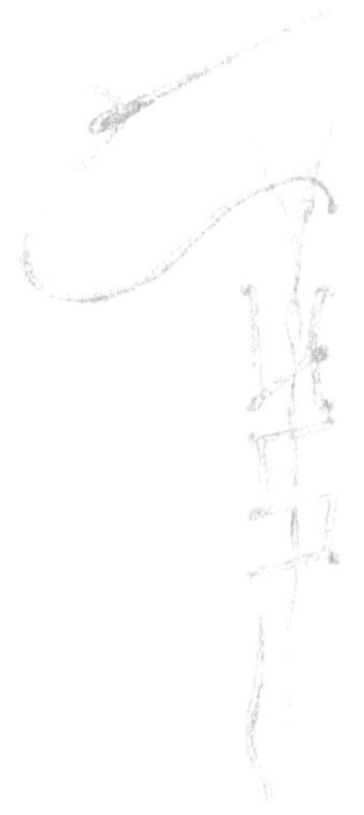

When the light begins to fray,
Splitting open
From the many faults of US
—that seam of dark through which the devils look to descend—
Only with every thread,
With every fiber,
All made from the truths
Of every man,
Woman,
And child,
Can that tear
Be sewn together again.

I think of the old songs of my wild youth,
Those childlike melodies that I so often replayed,
Like monotonous broken ballerinas in music boxes,
I hid them away throughout the years,
Lay buried in marked placed
Beneath the shallow sand of my mind.
I visit the beach from time to time,
Digging them up like little treasure chests.
I sit there by the shore.
I slowly open them all.
I close my eyes.

I shut out the roar of the distant waves
—the tempest of my adulthood—
And feeling the soft sand beneath my toes,
I listen.

They were the sweet sounds of my mother,
Her lullabies that sang me to sleep,
They were the encouraging tones of my father,
Running with my kite in the wind.
All the majestic sounds of my life
That would always be with me,
Becoming part of my own great songs,
Which one day
—not long from now—

I will leave behind,

scattered

across

the beaches

of loved ones.

Her eyes held the light
Of a thousand dying stars,
And the outline of her shadow
shimmered silver as she danced,
Swaying beneath the pale face
Of her old mother,
Moon.

She saw it all anew,
The shapes of herself molding to her emotion,
Fitting into her view of the world.
And within those spaces of her discovered,
She poured all the colors of her life,
Vibrant and dull,
Splashes and fine strokes,
Wanting to be it all,
To exist in ever-shifting feeling.
And by the rhythm of her heart beats,
Erratic and regular,
She would step to the song,
Heading off into the great beyond of her
—a woman.

We are constantly urged to love,
As our souls know too well
Of the fear that is felt without it.

Unlike a rainbow
Or the northern lights,
Allow your colors
To shine within the dark
As well as the day
… You are the constant light.

A great love,
At its end,
Never truly leaves you.
It bursts from such
Profound pain,
Scattering in
A million pieces,
Embedding deep
Within your soul.

It was in that space
Between heaven and earth
Where my love for you formed,
Where matter of emotions
Pressed into diamonds
… Hearts collide.

Having faith
In your dreams
Is looking up
And seeing the stars
In the middle of the day.

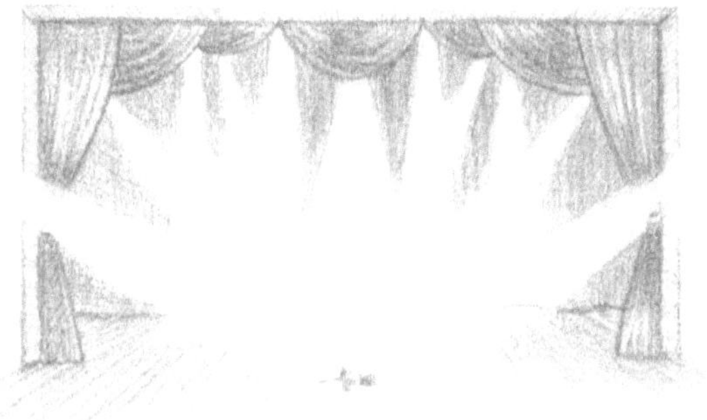

A new love takes your hand,
Lifting you back onto the stage,
Conversing in sweet tones of truth,
Gently reminiscing of pain
Before breaking into songs of joy.

… The performance of a lifetime,

Roses

Flung

At your feet.

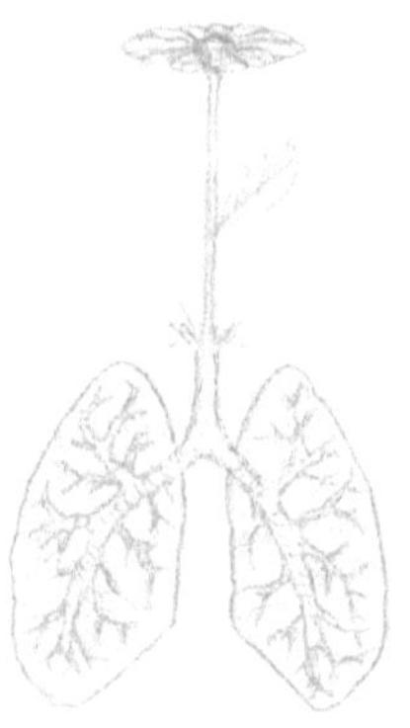

Place your ear
To the rising
Chest of the world.
You just may hear it,
The sound of all
These busy hearts
Beating in a silent
Symphony of love.

People often say how small they feel when standing upon a mountain,
Peering over the great ranges that stretch to the horizon.
I always felt bigger when making the perilous climb,
Lifted to the great heights of majestic peaks that pierced the sky.
Living amongst a swarm of suits is what always made me feel small,
Cities abuzz with false promises of more.
But there,
Above the noise
—the squabble to own it all—
The sprawling silence
Of the mountain
Settles my
Soul.

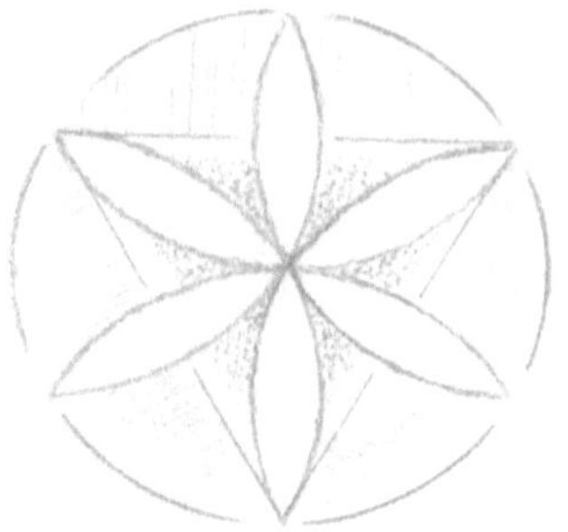

She was a crafter of dreams,
Stitching them together
Like cherry blossoms on paper trees,
Pulling threads of those that did not survive
The harsh winter winds of reality.
She still cared for them,
Those furled flowers,
Gathering them in bunches
Beneath her origami tree.
And like a child,
She would fall into that messy bed of her head,
Drifting off to sleep,
Weaving new dreams
That would bloom with the spring.

When we laugh,
And sing,
And dance,
It is our soul
Rejoicing
In the love
That it shares.

It is how her first love had grown,
The first she had come to know,
Weightless as it swelled,
Raising her up
Like helium balloons,
As she hoped to reach the moon.

The meeting
Of a soul mate
Is believing
In a divine contract,
Drafted by angels
—the language of love—
Signed by God.

'Break it if you dare
... Hmm, is that why they call it a broken heart?'

My heavy anchored heart
I haul from the sand,
My tempest soul I settle,
Once shaken by the raging sea.
I am at peace now,
No longer fighting the currents,
My life raft adrift,
Guided by my heart's compass.
And when cast upon a wayward shore,
I will accept the earth with a grateful heart,
Planting myself in all,
Like God,
Love abloom.

And at here at the end,
Where something new is to begin,
Where who you were before
Meets the first of many you will become,
Be grateful for what has been,
As the future will become the past,
And never again will you remain the same.

Blind is the man who looks upon a stream,
All a glimmer with colored clouds,
And only sees his reflection staring back.
Deaf is the woman who sits beneath the trees,
All a melody with the song of birds,
And only hears her troubled thoughts.

Take heed of false kings,
As we all shall rule
With mighty,
Rebellious beauty.
Take heed of those who mask the truth
With elegant lies,
As we all shall weigh their words
Against our own.
Take heed of ravenous wolves
Disguised as shepherds
Come to tend the flock,
As well shall bite back.
And lastly,
Do not take heed,
But take care of those whose hearts are true,
As we all shall share our love
With the kind
And courageous many
... Not few.

With every atom of knowledge we discover,
May we use this understanding of life to better our love,
To strengthen our bond,
Not just to learn for the purpose of expanding our minds.
And when we find ourselves drifting further away,
Our eyes set upon distant stars,
Our minds light years from home,
May we be guided back to *US*,
Through the light,
Through the years,
To when we took our first breath,
When our mothers first spoke our names,
Welcoming us into the world.

The deepest desire
Of our hearts
Is to dare
To love deeply.

From the top of a tall tree,
I gaze out across the land,
Seeing the endless possibilities
From the eyes of a younger me.
I stay a while,
Perched high among the shivering leaves,
Waiting for the day's last light to wane,
And in that moment,
As the sun dipped behind the sea,
Before the present calls me home
Like a worrisome mother,
I swear it was my future I glimpsed,
—an outline of my dreams.

99

She had a vagabond soul,
A gypsy girl reading palms,
Playing her tin plate tambourine,
Pockets filled with gold dust,
A heart full of dreams.

FIRST FLIGHT

She sings to the sea of her soul,
A weary sirens call,
And returning to the earthly shores of her mind,
Basking on a rock for all to see,
She shares the pearls of her truth,
Found deep within her depths,
Where no man
—as hard as they may try—
Could ever reach.

You,
My dear,
Possess that light
—A luminescence of love—
And it shall be my guide,
As I breathe my last breath,
As my heart beats its final beat
… Into the afterlife.

'On those clear nights,
Do you remember the ones?
Those we shared in the moonlight,
Laying beneath the stars,
Our backs wet with dew.
We tried our best to wish upon them all,
Drawing constellations in our minds,
Feeling the universe betwixt our palms,
Hands clasped,
Our imaginations entwined.

I lie here now,
On this night,
Alone,
Without you,
Looking up from the same patch of grass,
On the same hill,
Above the same little town
where we stumbled upon our love.
I think on those moments,
Those revenants of the old us scattered in the heavens,
Caught in the invisible net strung between the stars.

I sense you there,
The residue of you left like a trail of stardust,
Your soul streaking across the sky.
I close my eyes,
Wishing upon that shooting star,
Upon you.
I ask if one day
—after I live this life that I still need to live—
I may join you once more.
You will be faster than me,
As you always were,
Running off down the bank for home.
I will catch up,
gliding alongside you in a nebula
—a field of colored light—
And I will say:

"Let us take it all with us,
every moment before,
every moment after,
remembering everything,
forgetting nothing,
our love forever shining bright.'"

Her soul had come from the cosmos,
Made of magic and starlight.
Her heart had grown here on Earth,
Formed from water,
Wind,
And fire
… Ever wild.

107

If it is true that God is an artist,
With His brush that paints the sky,
Then Mother Nature is His muse.

G a r e t h   M a s s e y

'for Tarryn'

Your soul
Is a timeless
Work of art,
My love.
If only I could
Capture it on canvas,
Displayed in a glass case
… It would draw a crowd
In the Louvre
That would make
Mona Lisa blush.

I found my lover's star,
Remembering its spot in the sky
Like a seasoned sailor upon high seas.
I had to leave the city to find it,
Journeying back to the countryside.
It was such a dainty thing she had picked,
Calling it hers when pointing it out
On the night we first met.
I never quite felt it suited her,
As to me,
She was the kind of star
That hid in the heavens,
Concealing its beauty,
Like a shy shooting star,
Waiting to streak across the sky
On overcast nights.

Not needing to settle down with all the rest.
　And even if it tried,
　　If *she,*
　　　My young love,
　　　　Had so desperately hoped
　　　　　To find her place among the stars,
　　　　　　She never would,
　　　　　　　Simply destined to be so much more
　　　　　　　　… The galaxy's sapphire,
　　　　　　　　　Rarer than all its diamonds.

Imprint your purpose
On this world
Like a lipstick-stained kiss
Upon a napkin.

Angels do not fly,
They ride the light.
We are the ones who wish for wings,
Desperate dreamers with hopes
To reach the sun like Icarus.
Dream those seemingly impossible dreams,
Open your heart to the heavens,
Letting out a light
Bright with love.
An angel will come,
Swiftly upon your shine,
And she will show you how to glide,
To ride that never-ending light,
The one that begins at your heart,
Beaming out through the eternity of life.

Endless riches we cultivate
From the depths of our soul.
In the day,
These precious gifts are held close to our hearts
So others may easily see our wealth,
In the night,
They are placed under our pillow
So we may sleep upon sweet dreams of them.
Come the morning,
They are taken like teeth
—not by fairies but by angels—
Carrying a divine currency
Back home to the heavens.

She was reborn
With the spring,
Her heart sprouting
Hummingbird wings,
Beating furiously,
Shapeshifting
—infinity signs—
Suckling sweet nectar
Of the bountiful bliss
That blossomed
Beneath her.

I find myself standing here
At the corner of my street,
The end of a long road,
Blissful silver-gray.
I peer up as giant balloons pass by,
My childhood drifting past skyscrapers,
The colossal cartoon characters
Peeking through windows,
Searching for smiling children.
The confetti from cannons settles at my feet,
The music of marching bands wane,
And I look back from the corner of my street,
Seeing all who waved at me
When I was once atop my float.
I am ready now,
The parade of my life having drawn to a close,
But not my last performance,
Taking the show on the heavenly road.
And I fly,
Departing from my home
At the corner of my street,
Leaving bits of glitter
Stuck to my cheek.

May we cheat our demise,
 That when we pass,
Our life is embedded in the ones we love,
Like a pressed flower in a frame,
A memory preserved,
Its beauty living on.

Such wonders we are,
Loving fierce and frightful,
Shaped fragile and rare,
Like sand struck by lightning,
Made into dazzling wind chimes.

'God hangs us all outside his door,
Sitting on his porch,
—the rising dawns of the earth—
Listening to the sound of our songs.'

Tend to a wounded heart
As you would the injured wing of a bird,
With patience,
Hope,
And delicate care.
In time the heart will heal,
As any broken bone will do,
Never quite the same,
Yet stronger than before.
Love,
Like the bird,
With courage and grace,
Spreads its wings,
Taking to the sky,
Free to soar once more.

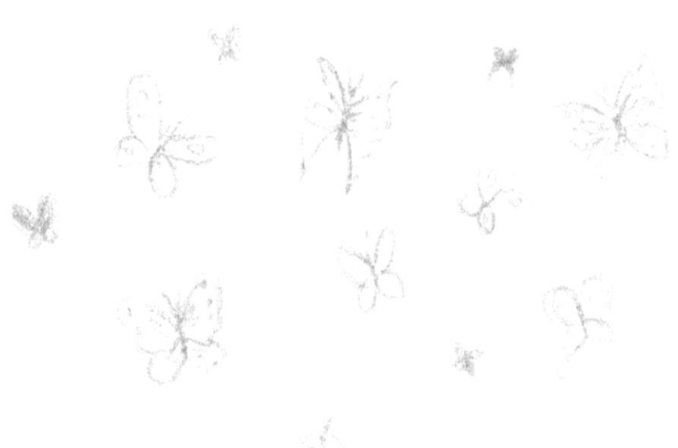

Her imagination was a flutter
Of a thousand butterflies,
A collage of colors
Dancing in the wind,
Which would one day settle
Upon the pages of the books
That she was born to write.

His legs burned,
Bounding through the scorched field.
They set fire to it for buds to grow,
Encouraging new life.
It felt the same for him,
As if someone set fire to his soul,
And like a Phoenix,
He was born anew,
Rising from the ashes
—the pain of his past scattered to the winds.

'Write your own story,'
She told me.
'It would surely be one worth telling.
God himself would not be able to put it down.
But could I give you a little advice,
from one writer to another,
from one life to another?'
I nodded.
'When crafting your masterpiece,
Be sure to fill the pages with others.
It is not an autobiography you are writing.
It is more in keeping of a great novel,
In need of compelling characters.
—the quirky,
The fearless,
The hopeful,
The faithless,
The brave,
The beautiful,
And blemished.
And for those whom you dearly love,
The ones most precious to you,
Pen them with words that sing,
With passages of sweeping prose,
Bringing you to laugh,
To cry,
To love,
To find comfort in.

And as difficult as it may be,
Pressing the pencil hard to paper,
The little indentations left like scars,
Write in those who have hurt you,
Never to tear those pages out,
As they too must be remembered,
The lessons we needed to learn.
And lastly, be generous with your words.
Your story is meant to be shared,
To be read by all who seek the beauty and knowledge they hold,
All who dare to be moved by all that is you.
They will take pieces of your loves and pains,
Carrying them wherever their path may lead,
And along the way,
Through the telling of their own story,
They shall also speak of yours.'
There was a moment of silence as she paused,
Thinking on her husband who had passed,
And wiping the tears from her cheek,
She softly spoke her last words...
'We are all stories,
Lives adjoined,
Flowing into one another,
Everlasting tales,
Standing the test of time.'

Your life is a story
Not in need of a rewrite.
It is perfectly flawed
And flawlessly perfected
To be nothing less than
What it was always meant to be.

A heart cannot truly break,
Yet it may fracture.
And when it does
—as it surely shall do in this life—

Allow love

To seep

Through

The cracks.

Write the story of your life
With boundless passion,
As if penned with a quill
Plucked from the wing
Of an angel.

Dreams are heroes of passion,
The daredevils of desire,
Risking death to reach the stars
… Do not look down.

After many years of carelessly creating,
I still find myself finger painting,
My hands stained with all colors of life,
Never wanting to pick up a brush.

EPILOGUE

An old woman told me a story once
Of an angel she had met
When sitting alone beside a stream,
And I thought it fair to tell her the tale of mine,
—the lady in white and lilac—
Who everyone said
I must have dreamed.

'It was in North Dakota,
Ten years ago,
When she came to me,'

I said to the woman,
Frowning at the wilting flower behind her ear.
'I was sitting in the shade of a cottonwood tree,
Beside the dried-up creek,
Once full and flowing
Like your glistening stream,
But there was not much water back then,
Thanks to the great drought of ninety-three.'
'Mine did not show himself to me,'
She replied with a sigh.
'I thought them shy,
Angels hiding in plain sight.'
'Well, she did keep her back to me,'

I explained,
'Kneeling beside the dried-up creek.
So maybe you are right,
And their faces of light
Are simply too bright for you and me.'
'Were you lost, back then?'
The woman asked.
'When you were sitting beneath your tree,
As I was beside my stream?'
'I was indeed,'

I replied,
'Accepting who I believed myself to be
—a selfish man free from the love
Of my friends and family.
But then she came,
Catching me plucking out the last of my loves,
Like the balls of cotton from the trees.
"I love them not,"
I told myself for each,
Basking in the glory of sweet love's defeat.'
'But now you love,'
The woman smiled.

'It is what that ring around your finger means.
It must have been something she did,
Something she said that made you see,
That made you believe in angels and love,
That something waited for you
Beyond that dried-up creek. '
'She did all that, '
I nodded.

'But with not so many words,
Not like that chatterbox angel of yours.
She simply kneeled there beside the creek,
Holding a clump of cotton in her hand
—one she must have plucked from the tree—
And in a whisper,
I heard her speak.
She said there was a drought in me,
Speaking of my dried-up shriveled heart of ninety-three,
And she placed the ball of cotton in a small puddle
—the last of the water from the creek.

She said,
"This is one of your loves,
One you have not yet plucked.
It is that of your mother,
And the water is her love for you.
She is soaked in that love,
Filled with it for all time.
It is the same with your heart,
Though you might think it has run dry."
I raised myself up out of the dry leaves,
And I said to her,
"I did not know that I had any love left.
My soul feels as baron as this dried-up creek."'
'What then? What did the angel say?'
The woman's eyes grew wide.

I replied,
'The truth of it,
As she told me,
Was...
"As it is with all life,
So it is the same with love,
And the clouds that darken the light within
Is not without the rain.
You are simply numb to the drops on your face.
You will feel it again."
She left me not long after,
And I stayed a while,
Sitting in her spot beside the almost dried-up creek.
I picked up the soaked ball of cotton,
Placing it in the breast pocket
Of my dusty shirt,
And I could feel it,
The love for my mother
Bleeding into my not so
Shriveled heart.'

Go forth…
And love lavishly.

Let's stay connected!
You can find me on Instagram:

@GARETH.W.MASSEY

Follow for updates and more about
my creative journey.